Opposites

Hard
and Soft

Siân Smith

Heinemann
LIBRARY

Chicago, Illinois

Edited by Siân Smith, Diyan Leake, and Brynn Baker
Designed by Tim Bond and Peggie Carley
Picture research by Elizabeth Alexander
Production by Victoria Fitzgerald
Originated by Capstone Global Library Ltd

Library of Congress Cataloging-in-Publication Data
ISBN 978-1-4846-0333-8 (paperback)
ISBN 978-1-4846-0348-2 (ebook PDF)

Printed in the United States of America
215

Acknowledgments
We would like to thank the following for permission
to reproduce photographs: Alamy: Design Pics
Inc., 16; Getty Images: Daniel Grill, 7, Jose Luis
Pelaez Inc, 6, Michael Wildsmith, 4, Tamara Murray,
9, 22b; Shutterstock: aperturesound, 21 left, Brian A
Jackson, 14, 22a, cristovao, front cover left, f9photos,
13, Gordan, front cover right, JI de Wetre-research,
12, JIANG HONGYAN, 8, 21 right, back cover top,
Madlen, 20 left, Mariusz Szczygiel, 18, mexrix, 5, back
cover bottom, Pavel Ignatov, 20 right, roroto12p, 11,
SoulCurry, 10

Every effort has been made to contact copyright
holders of material reproduced in this book. Any
omissions will be rectified in subsequent printings
if notice is given to the publisher.

Contents

Hard and Soft

A brick is **hard**.

A feather is **soft**.

The bat is hard.

The pillow is soft.

The hammer is hard.

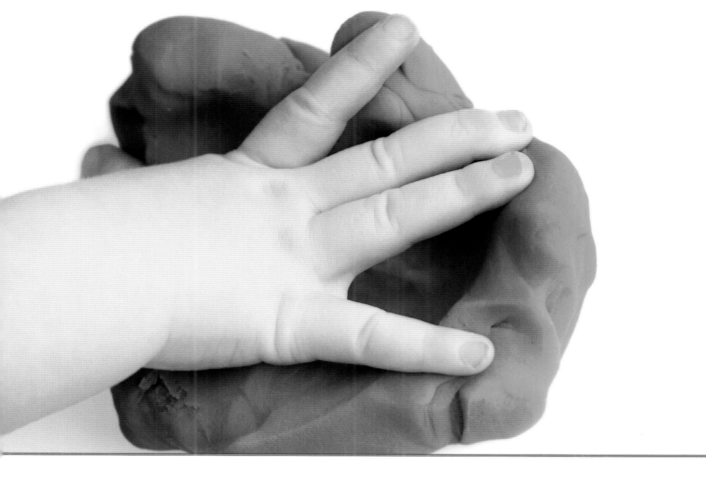

The play dough is soft.

A fork is hard.

A sponge is soft.

The shell is hard.

The sand is soft.

Is this ball hard or soft?

The ball is hard.

Is this bubble hard or soft?

The
bubble
is soft.

Is this hat hard or soft?

The
hat is
hard.

Hard and Soft Quiz

Which of these things are hard?

Which of these things are soft?

Answers on page 22

Picture Glossary

 **hard** solid and firm

 **soft** easily pressed or bent into a different shape

Index

Answers to questions on pages 20 and 21

The bolts are hard.
The blanket is soft.